One Loving Wish

Written by **Becca Sofia**

Illustrated by
Maria Kuchynskaya and Becca Sofia

Published by Little & Big LLC, New York

Cover design and illustrations by: Becca Sofia and Maria Kuchynskaya

Hardback ISBN-13: 978-1-955024-05-1
Paperback ISBN-13: 978-1-955024-01-3
eBook ISBN-13: 978-1-955024-02-0

Library of Congress Control Number: 2022914941
ISBN-13: 978-1-955024-05-1

Prep For Reader

One Loving Wish was written for parents with children aged three to six years old to help encourage dialogue around pregnancy loss and grief. It can be read to younger children based on the parent's judgment. At the end of this book, you will find advice that the author learned while going through pregnancy loss.

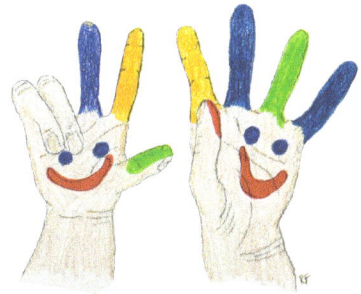

Author Dedication

In a room of 100 women, 10 to 20 have suffered at least one miscarriage. This book is dedicated to them and their loving wishes for a baby.

What do children, parents, and grandparents say?

"When I'm sad, I like to bike really, really, fast. It helps to put the sad into the wind." —Michael F, five years old.

"I didn't know what to tell our three-year-old daughter when we had first-trimester miscarriages. I never had a baby bump, so she only heard about it after the fact and would notice how sad we were. I could tell by my daughter's expression that she wanted to know. One Loving Wish gave us the courage to put words to our emotions." —Helena S.

"I gave One Loving Wish *to my grandson when my daughter suffered multiple miscarriages. It helped tremendously to work through our grief and guided us as grandparents on how to give support. This is not a topic that is discussed openly, and many women suffer in silence. The author Becca Sofia is brave to share her story, and we admire all the love-filled messages in this book." —Anna L.*

Birds chirp in every tree, and a fragrance of summer blossoms travels through the air.

Aya Rose and Mommy climb the treehouse staircase. It's time to play!

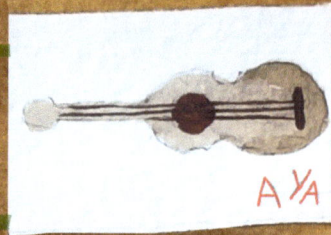

Aya sorts the colorful fruits and says, "Yummy for my tummy. Here, Mommy!"

"Oh, thank you, a banana!" Mommy pretends to nibble.

When Aya looks out the window, she sees her favorite animal and bursts with excitement, "A bunny!"

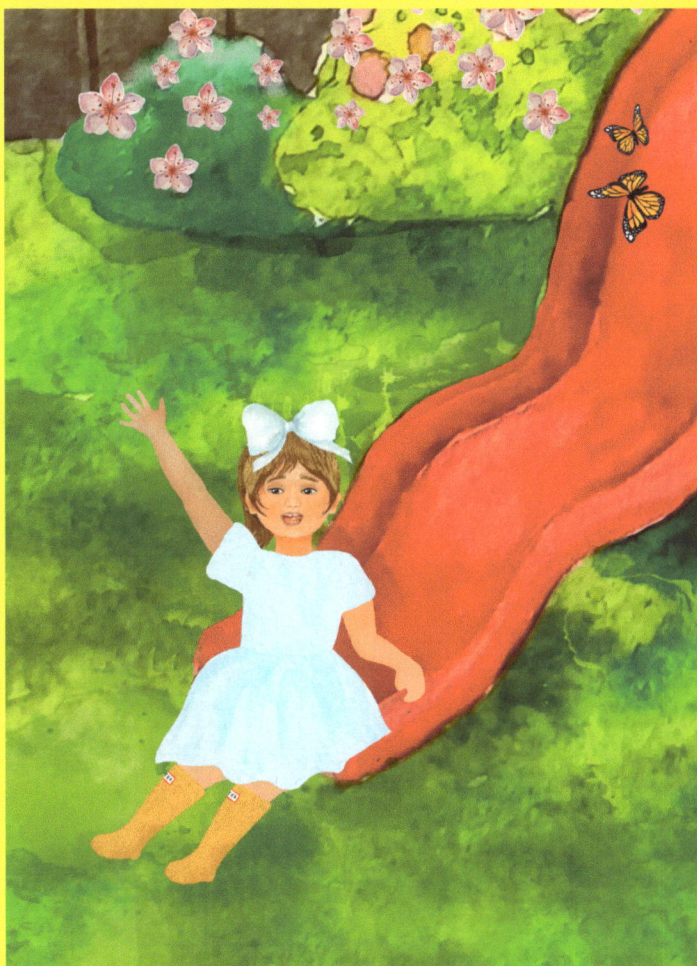

They rush down the slide, but the bunny has disappeared when their yellow rubber boots hit the grass.

Mommy sees Aya's searching gaze and steers her attention to the garden beds.

Their delightful garden is home to tomato plants, fresh herbs, and smiling sunflowers.

Mommy points at a sunflower and asks, "Aya, what color is this?"

Aya shines with pride and says, "Lellow!"

She thinks most things are yellow these days.

LADYBUG crossing

Summer passes by and brings colder days. Mommy wishes for a brother or sister for Aya, but they have waited a long time.

Mommy sits down with Aya and says,

"Sometimes, when you want something,
and you want it right now,
it takes a little longer or much longer somehow.
The waiting can make you worried; will it ever come?
You look for signs and movement, even if it's some.
This feeling is called *longing*."

Leave room in your garden for the fairies to dance

One morning in November, when Aya wakes up, Mommy is not there. Instead, she hears the warm voice of Grandma, "Good morning, sweet pea!"

After breakfast, Mommy and Daddy arrive home. Tears are falling down Mommy's cheeks. Her chin quivers, and she is unable to speak. It worries Aya. She fears Mommy is in pain and hugs her tightly.

Mommy explains, "I have big feelings right now. We just got back from the hospital. I want you to know that I'm okay and so happy to see you."

They sit down together. Daddy says slowly, "Mommy and Daddy are sad because Mommy had a tiny baby in her belly. It stopped growing and couldn't be born."

"This can sometimes happen, just like the sunflowers in our garden. They start as seeds, but some don't grow into flowers."

Aya asks,
"No baby?"

Mommy nods tearfully, "No, this baby didn't grow big
enough to be born and live outside of Mommy's tummy.
When you were in Mommy's tummy, you grew and grew,
and then you were born. We love you so much!"

One thing that can help sadness is spending time as a family. Mommy and Daddy know how much Aya loves hearing stories and cuddling, so they both tuck her into bed that evening.

Aya is all snug and comfy in the big bed. Daddy reads her favorite story while Mommy plays with Aya's hair.

Aya asks questions about the tiny seed that didn't grow; Mommy explains and adds, "We can be sad about the seed, but just like in the garden, we can plant another one. We have a chance to try it again."

Daddy says gently, "We might be sad for a while, and that's okay. We are a family and stay together."

Aya lovingly says, "Mommy is here, Daddy is here, Aya is here."

Dear friends can also help sadness; one day, some come over to play. Aya receives two gifts: a zebra mask and a box of colorful crayons.

Aya draws a big heart, and when she sees Mommy returns from rest, she says, "Mommy is back," and hands her the card.

Mommy's tear-filled eyes sparkle, and she says, "Yes, my love, I did some self-care. I rested my body, then had a nice shower. I love your drawing; what's your favorite part?"

"All the colors!" Aya exclaims.

Many months pass by, and it's summer again. When Aya and Daddy come home from school, they see Mommy in the blue chair.

Daddy checks in on Mommy, "Are you okay?"

Filled with emotion, Mommy says, "I'm okay. I'm crying because I miss the baby. You know, even when I'm sad, I'm still your Mommy who loves being with you." She pauses briefly, then continues, "Do you want to go outside and play?

They step out to their blooming garden and look who is hopping right in front of them – Bunny!

Mommy smiles and has a softness on her face.

Aya cheerfully says, "Mommy is not sad anymore."

They look up at the sky and see a rainbow.

Mommy bubbles up with love and says, "We trust the magic of new beginnings."

Aya smiles and says, "You are MY Mommy."

A note to caregivers

The author of this book suffered four pregnancy losses in one year, closely witnessed by their 2-year-old son. They happened at 13-, 9-, 8-, and 6 weeks gestation. The fourth one was an ectopic pregnancy resulting in emergency surgery. Becca could tell that her son had questions, and it was hard for her to find the right words. She did extensive research, talked to thought leaders, and eventually wrote this book for him and all other children witnessing loss in their families.

Looking back on that challenging year, the author can attest to how difficult situations can motivate you as a parent to find answers on how to best guide your child. Trust this instinct; you know what works best in your family to get back on track. In this book, the author highlights things that helped her family: self-care, bedtime bonding, reading books, playing outside, and receiving support from meaningful relationships. Remember, you are not born to be a perfect parent; you can only grow together.

Child Development Specialist, Laura Araman, hosted an excellent talk at the school of the author's son. One message she highlighted was Mr. Fred Rogers' heartwarming quote, "All children need to see that adults in their lives can feel big emotions and not hurt themselves or anyone else when they feel that way." During the summer of 2022, the author read an inspiring social media post by Dr. Becky Kennedy (@drbeckyatgoodinside), saying, "Early experiences of connection around distress leave a child more resilient and able to cope with hard things." Dr. Kennedy has a wealth of knowledge about parenting, and she breaks it down into relevant and valuable steps.

Another favorite resource of the author is Louise Hallin, a Swedish midwife, and therapist with hundreds of hours of podcast advice to parents. She says, "Decades of research shows that when a child is experiencing a distant and sad parent, their response is often to become clingier and to regress. They might negatively seek your attention, pee in their pants, or stop using a spoon and eat with their hands." The truth is, there is no bad kid, only a kid having a hard time. If you hide your sadness, even with good intent to protect them from something that hurts, chances are your child will still know something is up. Developmental Psychologist Dr. Gordon Neufeld says, "Children do not experience our intentions, no matter how heartfelt. They experience what we manifest in tone and behavior."

"A rainbow baby" is an extended term of a healthy baby born after a miscarriage, infant loss, or stillbirth. It is a beautiful reminder that a rainbow typically follows a storm; similarly, rainbow babies give love and light after a period of darkness. The author hopes this book can be one of your many forms of support.

One Loving Wish summarizes five pieces of advice:

1. Engage in self-care
2. Turn towards (not away)
3. Welcome your child's questions and emotions
4. Nourish meaningful relationships
5. Practice gratitude

1. Engage in self-care

The author advises you to pause, take a deep breath, and check in with your body. What feelings come up? What do you need? Engaging in self-care has been clinically proven to reduce stress and depression and improve happiness. Like an airplane's oxygen mask, help yourself before helping others. Think about ways that allow you to be a loving leader for your child. As you get stronger, your child will mirror your growth.

The author and her husband started couples therapy during their year of loss. It helped tremendously to channel their emotions and to focus on the bigger picture (rather than just on the losses). Check out the "Gottman method." Becca also joined a pregnancy loss group of five women that met virtually twice per month, and the group was moderated by a therapist focusing on pregnancy loss. You can find this type of group via your OBGYN. The author received so much support and wisdom from the other women. After about a year, the group ended with some being pregnant again and others deciding to stop trying. Most importantly, each group member left uniquely feeling gratitude and support. That feeling inspired the author to end this book not with a second baby but rather with the message, "One loving wish to come together."

The author also found it helpful to learn many self-soothing techniques. Everyone is different, so find what feels suitable for you at the moment, e.g., a hot shower, listening to music, eating a healthy meal, going for a walk, or playing an instrument. A wise 5-year-old inspired the author with "The five-finger breath." It involves using your index finger to trace your fingers on your other hand. Breathe in on the upward movement along the finger, breathe out on the downward, then move on to the next finger.

2. Turn towards (not away)

Let your child know that it's okay to cry, that our tears tell us that our body has an important feeling. You can highlight that this type of tear is my sadness, but tears can also mean other emotions, such as fear, joy, frustration, etc. Give your child the tools to label their own and others' feelings. The author thinks this is also true for partners; try the loving gesture of turning towards, repeating back what you just heard your partner describe. With time, this practice can help couples work together through loss. The author is not saying to share every moment of tears, instead, be mindful and try to minimize times when you are distancing yourself from your child or partner.

When you are deep in thought and want to explain, the author found it helpful to say, "Mommy is thinking." Louise Hallin advises, "When you don't have the words, close body contact while rocking your child back and forth is better than turning your back on them."

A powerful tool around young children is to show hands for the concept of time. For example, form a space between two hands and say, "I have cried for this long, and I wish for a little bit more time to finish crying" (moving hands to a smaller space). Aya's mom favors the blue chair, where she lets go of emotions. Think about a place that feels good for you.

3. Welcome your child's questions and emotions

Start with, "I want to talk about something that may bring up big feelings for all of us." Talk slowly, use short sentences with your child and make eye contact; This maintains connections and helps a child feel safer. Aya's dad shares the news about the tiny baby that stopped growing and couldn't be born. Allow the message to sink in, and questions may come later. Keep in mind every child can react differently. Stay open-minded and know that reactions can come at different times. Sometimes making simple drawings together can help explain complex topics.

The author rewrote the section explaining the pregnancy loss so many times. The result includes many conversations with the resources listed at the end of the book. At one point, the author spoke with Edy Nathan, psychotherapist and thought leader grief and trauma, who shared the importance of being precise and avoiding indirect words. For example, "The baby is in a restful sleep" can implant a fear of sleep, or "We lost the baby" may trigger your child to think you can lose them too. The message is to be mindful of how the child may interpret something. Try to pause and wait for your child's questions.

4. Nourish meaningful relationships

Aya's parents have grandma and friends come over to their home. Ask for help and accept it when it's offered. Grief is a personal process; the author remembers gravitating to her closest circle, especially right after each loss. Eventually, the valuable phrase "lean forward" made sense. It could relate to her thoughts, actions, or favorite people. It became a mantra, and looking back, she grew as a person little by little.

This book focuses on the parents caring for their children during times of loss. The author remembers how helpful it was to stick to a regular bedtime routine with her son. Routine aids in better sleep and self-help skills. Reading to your child is another powerful way to create a connection. Louise Hallin is a believer in skin-to-skin contact, just like at birth when you hold your child for the first time. It gives you comfort and releases the hormone oxytocin, which boosts well-being. Mimic this with your child during challenging times by embracing them during a bath or story time. Louise Hallin says, "Do this for up to two weeks or until your child shows signs for you to stop, or they might ask you to read a story instead." Your child may also say, "I'm not a baby," and then you know you have anchored the connection, at least for a moment.

5. Practice gratitude

Loss is partly tough because it makes you feel like you lose control. It's like watching your life unfold without you in it. The author found it helpful to focus on the things she could influence and grow gratitude around them. For example, caring for her body with exercise and a healthy diet, close relationships, gratitude around cute phrases her son would say, or simply practicing mindfulness in nature. Whatever makes you feel good, do more of those things. Studies have shown that writing down what we are thankful for stimulates our brains to feel more grateful. In the darkest times, gratitude may not come naturally but trust its impact. Remember, energy flows where attention goes. Grief is not a start and end point situation, but it will evolve, and so will you.

Here is a concluding quote by Jack Kornfield, author and one of the famous teachers of Buddhist mindfulness practice in the West. His podcast "Heart Wisdom" offers excellent spiritual guidance.

> "Grief is a long, tender process to digest little by little. Put a hand on your heart and hold yourself in tenderness. Tell yourself, may you be held in compassion. May your struggles and sorrows be eased. May your heart be at peace."
>
> —Jack Kornfield

The Last Word

Thank you for being open to hearing this story. Parents like you, who seek ways to strengthen relationships in your family, will change future generations for the better! We would love to hear from you, any thoughts, ideas, or comments, please email **books@littleandbig.com**. Thank you for spreading the word; the author would greatly appreciate it if you left a review.

LB LITTLE & BIG
LIVE | READ | PLAY

About the author

Becca Sofia is a writer, illustrator, and former Senior Horologist with deep knowledge of watch authentication and strategy. She was born in Sweden, studied in Australia, and lives in the U.S. One Loving Wish is her first book, which she wrote after experiencing recurrent pregnancy losses between her children. It aims to lift the stigma around early miscarriage and support difficult conversations with children. Her goal as an author is to spread the love of reading and to build support around parenting. Becca loves skiing on a fresh powder day in the Rocky Mountains, playing the piano, and dancing in colorful costumes. She lives in New York with her husband and children. Follow Becca on Instagram at @beccasofiabooks.

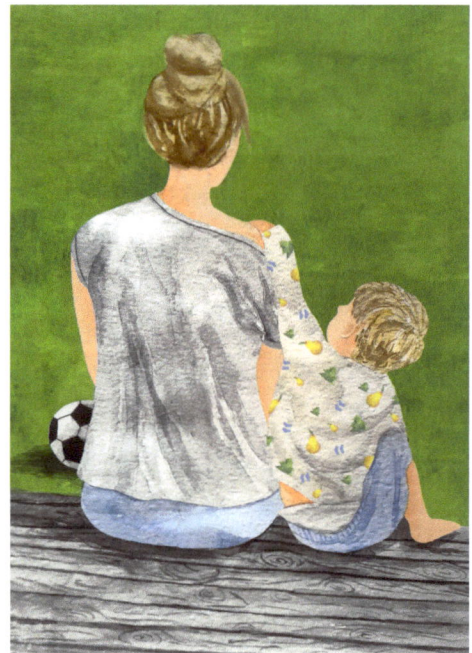

A difficult moment that ultimately led the author to write this book.

Recommended resources:

- Laura Araman, clinical social worker, LCSW, MSEd, SEIT, play therapist and child development specialist. New York, USA.

- Louise Hallin, nurse practitioner, midwife and psychotherapist. Stockholm, Sweden.
  www.louisehallin.se

- Dr. Becky Kennedy, Ph.D, psychologist, founder of Good Inside. New York, USA.
  www.goodinside.com

- Edy Nathan, MA, LCSWR, psychotherapist, thought leader grief and trauma, differentiation model. New York, USA.
  edynathan.com

- Dr. Gordon Neufeld, developmental psychologist, child development specialist. BC, Canada.
  neufeldinstitute.org

- Jack Kornfield, author, Buddhist practitioner. California, USA.
  www.jackkornfield.com

www.ingramcontent.com/pod-product-compliance
Lightning Source LLC
LaVergne TN
LVHW072059070426
835508LV00002B/175